PRAYING WITH UNDERSTANDING

Richard Dare Ajiboye

Richard Dare Ajiboye

INTRODUCTION

Christians, world over, place indescribable value on prayer. We pray before we sleep and pray when we wake up. We pray before we eat. We pray to God before commencing virtually everything. Before we get married, we pray for God's guidance to help us make the right choice of spouse. When we do get the right person to marry, we start praying on how to get a suitable date for the wedding and financial support to carry out the necessary activities and even a good weather on the day of the wedding. Thereafter, we start praying for the wife to conceive and when she does, safe delivery becomes our next target of prayer. After delivery, we start praying for the growth of the child physically, intellectually, spiritually, morally, career and eventually again for the child to be married to the right person and the cycle continues.

After the child has grown up and graduates from the university, he starts praying for a good job. When he gets one, he starts praying for career growth, security, success, among other issues of life. The cycle of prayer continues till we end our sojourn here on earth. It is obvious that one thing we can never get to do too much of is praying. One may eat too much, sleep too much, talk too much, read too much, among other things, but you may never get to pray too much.

The Bible says,

"Pray without ceasing" - 1 Thessalonians 5:17 (NKJV). The Bible also says, "He then told them a parable on the need for them to pray always and not become discouraged" (HCSB).

This passage teaches us the need to pray always. It also exposes the fact that we may not always get instant positive response when we pray hence the admonition not to get discouraged or grow faint.

The experience of Daniel further affirms that it is not every prayer that delivers the instant result. Daniel 10:12-13A says,

> *"Don't be afraid, Daniel, he said to me, for from the first day that you purposed to understand and to humble yourself before your God, your prayers were heard. I have come because of your prayers. But the prince of the kingdom of Persia opposed me for 21 days" (HCSB).*

There is a difference between God hearing prayers and giving answers to prayers. Daniel prayed for 21 days, and the answer was dispatched to him through an angel on the first day. However, the answer and the angel were withstood by the Prince of Persia for 21 days until Angel Michael intervened. Daniel got the desired answer on the twenty-first day, though it had been released on the first day of the prayer. When we pray in righteousness, God hears our prayers, but many factors could be responsible for delay in getting desired response. It is important for Christians to identify why answers to their prayers are delayed; it could be sin, doubt, wrong request, timing, Satan, among other factors. Knowing the root-cause of delayed answer will help re-strategising about how we pray.

We pray round the day as individuals and congregationally. Some Churches declare long days of praying and fasting to seek the face of God for one thing or another. We pray using all manners of approaches – prayer of thanksgiving, supplication, quiet or aggressive prayers and in whatever way you may want to talk about. You see all manners of books on prayers, but our world appears not to reflect the level of prayers we offer to God.

We have individuals and countries that do not believe in prayers, yet they prosper compared to individuals and countries that are so religious about prayer. What then is wrong? Is it that prayer is not necessary? Could it be that the ungodly have better sources of power than Christians? Is it that we do not know how to pray, or God has stopped answering prayers? These questions are not to promote prayerlessness, neither are they to cast doubt on the efficacy of prayer.

Obviously, the unrighteous may prosper for many reasons that we may not be able to discuss in this book. The devil has possessed them and will do everything to keep them busy with success that will distract them from doing God's will. Unbelievers may prosper because of some inherent demonic powers they possess, though such prosperity has strings attached as the devil has no free gifts. Unlike God who freely gave Jesus for our salvation, Satan gives to take back in multiple folds. You cannot receive from Satan and avoid giving back to him.

Furthermore, the ungodly may also prosper by following some biblical principles of success, which some believers may not pay attention to, even though they keep praying. The biblical principle of blessing as in Luke 6:38 has remained universally precise and accurate to deliver blessings to anyone who obeys the principle of giving. This is not about being a child of God or not. You give, you receive. I must be quick to say that God is still in the business of answering prayers. He may however choose to answer in the affirmative by saying yes or in the negative by saying no. He may also say yes but requires that you are patient to receive answer to your prayer request. In answer to prayers, there are times when God may choose to calm raging storm. He may choose to calm us, while He allows the storm to rage on. God could also choose to calm us and calm the storm also. Whichever, God has lessons for us to learn from the situations as we pray to Him.

As important as prayer is, some Christians still seem not to understand the essentials of effectively praying to God. If you are wondering about how and why, you may be surprised to note that even one of His disciples came to him requesting Him to teach them how to pray. In Luke 11:1,

> *"Now it came to pass, as He was praying in a certain place, when He ceased, that one of His disciples said to Him, Lord, teach us to pray, as John also taught his disciples." - (NKJV).*

Taking an analytical look at the text above, Jesus is a praying role model. Praying effectively actually requires learning some basic principles. Of course, the greatest teacher on how to pray is the Holy Spirit, but we need some basic understanding when we pray. One may be wondering why the disciples of Jesus asked to be taught how to pray having been with Him most of the time. They just saw Him praying and they asked for a lecture on how to pray.

Praying naturally should be like a relationship between a child and the father. Nevertheless, we should also ask ourselves why we pray at times without having the desired response to our prayers. Could it be that there are techniques of praying? Do we need any style or specific time and place to pray for God to answer our prayers? Could it also be that we lack the qualities required to effectively pray? We may also need to know if our prayers are not answered because we are praying outside the will of God for our lives. The following chapters in this book will help us understand how best to pray and pray effectively. Matthew 6:7-13 will be our main text as we discuss how to pray with understanding and effectively.

WHAT IS PRAYER?

What is the meaning of prayer? Since it is not a concept exclusive to Christians, we may need to take general perspectives of prayer. In the legal parlance, prayer means making a request to a judge about a civil or criminal case. It may be a prayer for justice on behalf of a plaintiff; a request for redress for unfair treatment meted out by an accused person on a plaintiff; a request by an accused person for a case against him to be quashed or set aside; or a plea for leniency by a defender.

Prayer may mean a request from someone to another person, i.e., a friend to a friend, a child to his parents, a wife to the husband, a subordinate to a superior in an office setting or vice versa. It may even be a request by a disadvantaged person like a beggar asking for help from a rich person. Prayer may also be defined as a request to God.

In addition, the word prayer according to the Strong's Concordance is derived from the Hebrew word *tehfilah* which appears in the Old Testament more than 75 times and could mean asking, begging, and supplication. Prayer is believed to be more than asking and begging. Therefore, some schools of thought believe that describing prayer from the point of view of asking alone is inadequate.

Lizorkin-Eyzenberg (2017), in Jewish Culture and History, said prayer is generally viewed in English as making request either to God or a person. However, prayer in the right perspective could be viewed from the point of introspection, which in Hebrew is primarily from the word *tehfilah*. Therefore, from this Hebrew word, prayer is conceptually described as bonding between God and man just as between a father and his child as an outcome of self-examination.

Looking at most of the definitions above, one may be tempted to think that prayer is a mono-directional exercise. But prayer is supposed to be a two-way communication between man and God, a dialogue and not a monologue. The process of the communication when praying requires that we talk with God and patiently wait to hear from Him. But most times we often want to impose our requests on God such that we only pour out our minds to Him but never wait to get His feedback.

As much as we may love petitioning God about what we want from Him, He is equally interested that we listen to Him before running away from His presence. Looking at prayer from a relationship model, I will define it as a mutual exchange of communication between two or more parties with the intention of getting attention or favour. However, the relationship with God when praying has defined parameters that enhance smooth interaction and getting positive results.

Every form of relationship has defined guidelines. This is one of the reasons people do not rush into a relationship without understanding its implications for the parties involved. Prayer is a continuous relationship with God, during and after the time of prayer. You need to keep your stand with God in holy alliance even when you are not praying. Prayer is not an activity but a process of relationship.

OUR FATHER IN HEAVEN

This is the longest chapter in this book. This is necessary for so many reasons, but essentially, it is foundational to praying effectively. In the response of Jesus Christ to the request of His disciples for a lecture on how to pray, He gave them as a pattern the popular prayer we often refer to as our Lord's Prayer. Jesus' teaching on prayer starts with "Our Father in heaven". What should we learn from this? It means prayer to God requires a relationship with Him, not just a creature-creation relationship, but a paternal relationship.

There is a magnitude of difference between being created by God and being His child. Most people end their relationship at the level of creator-creature even though they go to Church or bear Christian names. Without much ado, being God's creature is not by choice but becoming a child of God is by choice. In John 3:16, the Bible says,

> *"For God so loved the world, that He gave His only begotten Son, that whosoever believes in Him should not perish, but have everlasting life" (KJV).*

The believe factor in the above Bible verse is a choice one may decide to make or not make. God will never force anyone to believe in Jesus. The truth I want us to understand here is that effective prayer is rooted in a relationship that results from becoming a child of God through faith in Christ's crucifixion, death and resurrection. Any person, not minding his or her status in the Church or outside the Church, can pray and fast for days without being a child of God. However, praying without daughter- or sonship relationship with God renders such prayers mechanical and ritualistic.

The Bible says in Proverbs 12:22,

> *"Lying lips are abomination to the Lord: but they that deal truly are his delight" (KJV).*

Furthermore, in Proverbs 15:8 the Bible says,

> *"The sacrifice of the wicked is an abomination to the LORD: but the prayer of the upright is his delight" (KJV).*

A sinner can be described with many adjectives, one of it is a wicked person. So, praying to God as a sinner is irritant to Him except a prayer of repentance. We cannot be making too many requests with audacity to a man with whom we have no adoptive or biological relationship and expect him to treat us as his true children. You have limitations when it comes to relating with a benefactor who is not your father or mother.

Do not forget we are talking about understanding how to pray effectively here, that means, prayers that always achieve the purposes for which they are offered. I am not saying God does not listen to the prayer of a sinner outright, especially when a sinner turns to God in prayer with genuine repentance. In Joel, 2:12-13 the Bible says,

> *"Yet even now, declares the LORD, return to me with all your heart, with fasting, with weeping, and with mourning; and*

rend your hearts and not your garments. Return to the LORD your God, for He is gracious and merciful, slow to anger, and abounding in steadfast love; and he relents over disasters" (ESV).

The above verses again demonstrate the Fatherhood of God, but he hates sin. He, however, loves a sinner and does not want him or her to perish. When a sinner turns to God in prayer with full repentance, He is ever ready to listen to such prayer. However, to the prayers of unyielding and unrepentant sinner, God is un-interested. When sinners get things from God, it may be from the commonwealth blessings which some often misinterpret to be the results of their prayerfulness.

One does not just become a child by fantasising; you become a child either biologically or by adoption. Either of these will qualify you to become a child and have access to the rights of belonging to a family. Similarly, to call God your father must be through a process. The Bible says,

> *"For God loved the world, that he gave is only begotten Son, that whosoever believeth in him should not perish, but have everlasting life" – John 3:16 (KJV).*

Just as birth precipitates biological father-child relationship, so a spiritual father-child relationship between us and God must start with a birth. The Bible says in John 3:3,

> *"Jesus answered and said unto him, verily, verily, I say unto thee, except a man be born again, he cannot see the kingdom of God." (KJV).*

Becoming a child of God is by one's faith and decision to accept

Christ. Salvation is free, but you need a decision to accept Christ as your Lord and Saviour to actualise the grace of becoming a child of God. The Bible says,

> *"God is faithful, by whom ye were called unto the fellow-ship of his Son Jesus Christ our Lord" - 1 Corinthians 1:9 (KJV).*

Our heirship with Christ qualifies us for many things, one of which is unhindered access to God and this gives you the confidence to pray as a genuine child. The Bible says,

> *"And because ye are sons, God hath sent forth the Spirit of his Son into your hearts, crying, Abba, Father" - Galatians 4:5 (KJV).*

The spirit of adoption that we have through our salvation gives us boldness to approach the throne of grace in prayers. We enter a divine relationship with God when we become His children. This gives us unconditional access to Him.

To always pray effectively, there is need to understand that we need the first encounter with God as our father. Praying with any form of physicality and spiritual strategies without a constant connection with God as father amounts to seeking quick fixes in praying. There are no quick fixes in relating with God. You either get it right or not. True enough, we cannot deceive God. Being prayerful may project one as being spiritual and in right standing with God before people, but to God, it may amount to mere unrecognised rituals. We must turn our prayers to a relationship rather than a ritualistic disposition. Sonship is a must with God if we must pray effectively.

In Romans 8:16-17,

"The Spirit himself bears witness with our spirit that we are children of God, and if children, then heirs – heirs of God and fellow heirs with Christ, provided we suffer with him in order that we may also be glorified with him." – ESV.

This verse has stressed the importance of being in relationship with God as His children for effective prayers. A child is an heir apparent and simply has access to his father's property as a legitimate child. If we are heirs with Christ, it means we have gone through the rebirth experience, dead to sin and alive to righteousness.

Being an heir qualifies us for God's closet and close intimacy with Him by which we know His mind and always seek Him in everything before we are engrossed with possessing everything that is seemingly good. The Bible says in Philippians 2:5,

"Let this mind be in you, which was also in Christ Jesus." - KJV.

If we have Christ's mind, we will persevere and be patient in prayer. Longsuffering is one of the Christ-like minds we must have as Christians who wants to pray effectively.

A child who knows his father very well and how to relate with him will have unhindered access to his father and His wealth. Do we really know God, or do we see Him as Father Christmas with the way we pray to Him? Getting to intimately know a person does not happen by accident; it takes time and intentional effort. If that is the way it works with us as human beings, what makes us think it would be any different with God. It takes willingness, time, consistent and conscious effort to know God. This knowledge cannot but rub off on our prayer, as through intimacy, we get to know and pray in line with the mind and will of God.

Part of the price of our credentials as Christians, that qualifies us as God's children is the process He takes us through. This involves suffering for His work and some form of discipline. God takes us through the process to make us strong and help us stand. Some of the things we earnestly cry and pray for God to remove might just be part of the things we must suffer for the sake of God's kingdom. God's children are also God's army. He, therefore, takes us through His process to purge us and refine us so we can be in position to put the adversary to flight.

A true child of God must know when he is going through a trying time in his Christian journey. Philippians 3:10 says,

> *"That I may know him, and the power of his resurrection, and fellowship of his sufferings, being made conformable unto his death." - KJV.*

This does not mean that every hardship we go through must be termed as the trial of our faith. The devil has hidden under this guise to punish so many Christians. A true child must seek God's face to discern a situation like this. We may need to understand that delayed prayers sometimes may be one of the trials of our faith. It does not mean that being a child of God grants us yes to our prayers instanter all the time. The Bible says,

> *"Not only that, but we rejoice in our sufferings, knowing that suffering produces, endurance, and endurance, produces character, and character produces hope and hope does not put us to shame, because God's love has been poured into our hearts through the holy Spirit who has been given to us" - Romans 5:3-5 (ESV).*

Our sonship experience gives us character that produces godliness in us. Character is about who we really are which is different from our reputation which is about how people see us. Who we are may be different from how we are sometimes perceived by others. Who we are is how God perceives us. As children of God we must understand all these truth in our prayers.

We may deceive people with our high-sounding titles in the Church and eloquence in speech when we pray, but God, who is our creator and father to those who are regenerated, knows us and relates with us according to who we truly are. The character of Job in the Bible proved the qualities God flaunted to the devil. A godly character will make a child of God to remain faithful even when the answer to his or her prayer is delayed. No wonder Job says,

"Even if He kills me, I will hope in Him" - Job 13:15A (HCSB).

God's yes or no to His child's prayer does not make him or her misbehave. True children of God are firmly rooted in Christ, their relationship is not based on what they get from God. Their characters are formed to take whatever answer God gives to their prayers because they are confident that God's thoughts towards them are thoughts of good (Jeremiah 29:11). Therefore, the response of God's children to whatever answer He gives to their prayer is, "Let your will be done, oh Lord".

People run from one Church denomination to another in the name of seeking miracles. Is it that God is not present in all the places they have been to? Of course, people are receiving their miracles from God in the various denominations from where others may have left for another. We even pray dangerous prayers against our enemies. **I must say that what the children of God need is a holy life that is dangerous to their enemies and not dangerous prayers**. No wonder, most of such dangerous prayers are mere empty noise to God. If our lives are truly like that of God as His children, we would have been able to say by faith that this *mountain* should be moved and cast into the sea and it will be so.

I remember having a strong mountain before me in the early 1990s for which I had to turn to God for help. I was invited to minister in a secondary school during a severe fuel scarcity. The fuel of the motorcycle I was to use was on reserve tank. By experience, the reserve tank of that motorcycle would ordinarily not take me beyond about 7 kilometres. I prayed to God to help me go on a return journey for the ministration and that was about 20 kilometres. The best option for me and my assistant was to use the motorcycle since the fuel scarcity had taken almost all the commercial vehicles off the road. We embarked on the journey, I passed the seven kilometres, and got to the venue of the ministration, about 10 kilometres journey. We carried out the assignment and thereafter started our journey back home.

We rode back home and on getting to where I would park the motorcycle, it stopped by itself, of course the fuel had finished long ago. But I told my heavenly father what I wanted because of the condition beyond my control and He fuelled the motorbike divinely without fuel in the tank. You may term this a way of tempting God, but it was not. It was an era when there were no telephone services in our local communities; there was no opportunity to call to cancel the appointment. Because of the fuel scarcity, getting public transport was near impossibility and even if I got one to the venue, coming back would have been another challenge. God, my father took charge of the journey, even if it had to take the motorcycle running on *supernatural fuel*.

If you have not given your life to Christ as your personal Lord and Saviour, you may be one of the beneficiaries of God's benevolence as his creature. There are things you enjoy being God's creature and you will surely receive such general blessings either you pray or not. There are also principle-based blessings, tied to working and giving. You will receive blessings attached to such principles with or without prayers, barring satanic obstructions or manipulations. In Luke 6:38, the Bible says,

"Give, and it shall be given unto you; good measure, pressed down, and shaken together, and running over, shall men give into your bosom. For with the same measure that ye mete withal it shall be measured to you again." (KJV).

When you see unbelievers, who are not children of God having multiple blessings at times, it may just be connected to the principle of giving. Nevertheless, you may also see a fervent prayer warrior, born again languishing in poverty due to disobedience to the principle of giving and receiving. So, a child of God will not only pray, but must understand and apply kingdom principles to breakthrough.

If we see prayer from the point of view of asking and receiving alone, we may be missing a lot of things as God's children. Prayer as defined earlier should be based on relationship with God the Father. You do not hop off from your biological parents upon getting what you have asked from them. An effective prayer requires still depending on God for guidance on how to use what he has given to you.

Many people may have died prematurely just by being blessed and because they lacked maturity; they hopped off prematurely before God and run into destruction. When a true child asks his father for anything, he is equally delighted in pleasing his father with what has been given to him. When you are engaged in an effective prayer, you wait for your father to direct you on when, where and how to use whatever he has given to you in answer to your prayer. Timing, place and how you use God's blessing or given resources in answer to your prayers is paramount.

There are literary issues in the context of "our father in Heaven" as illustrated in the Lord's prayer taught by Jesus. Heaven is a holy place, a perfect place. This places a demand on us then that our lives pre, during and post praying to God should be a quintessence of holiness and aspiration for perfection. In walking with God in prayer, he requires that we live a life of holiness. The Bible says the eyes of God is holy and cannot behold evil or look on iniquity (Habakkuk 1:13). God told Abraham to walk before him and be perfect. Perfection is an achievable state by God's grace, but we have our part to play to attain this state of perfection.

Come to think of this, have you thought of the father/child relationship of a toddler? A child trusts his earthly father for everything. When we pray, the three **Ps** of faith must be understood. The first **P** = provision. A toddler has absolute trust in his or her father and will simply ask for anything without doubting the ability and the willingness of the father to supply what is requested. As a matter of fact, a child believes that the father has everything and all that is needed is to simply ask and then you receive. No wonder the Bible says ask and you will receive (Luke 11:9).

When my son was very young, my family got a Kia Cerato 2007 Model and he was happy to see it. One day we were driving to church, and he saw the latest model of the same car. He immediately detested ours and requested that I buy the latest model. Little did he know that I took a loan to buy the one we had and was still servicing the loan. At another time, he wanted not just a car again but a four-wheel drive Sport Utility Vehicle (SUV). There is no amount of explanation to such a young boy that will convince him that you cannot afford such a vehicle.

A young child simply believes his or her father can provide everything he or she asks for. Even though the reality is that earthly fathers lack the resources to provide just everything that the children ask for, young children simply believe their fathers have the capacity to provide anything they ask for. This is simple faith. When we pray to God, we need this type of radical faith like a baby who believes his or her father has everything and will give when we ask.

The second **P** is protection. There are difficult and life-threatening situations we pass through as God's children. It could be the need for protection from our enemies, spiritual and/or physical. If we have the faith of a toddler, we simply believe that God can deliver us when we pray. If a toddler is threatened by someone stronger than him/her, a bully, perhaps, he or she will simply tell the oppressor, "I will tell my daddy." A toddler believes that the father has the strength to ward off any form of aggression and protect him or her from any form of danger. When we are threatened by situations or people, take it to God in prayer by faith like a toddler will do.

The third **P** is partnership. This expresses the relationship that a toddler has with the father. No matter what, a child goes to the father unhindered and not with a beggarly disposition. When we are truly God's children, our approach when we pray should be that we are talking with our father. Let us look at the example of a strayed-dog and a pet-dog in a home. If a dog strays into your home, you are at liberty to give remnant food to it or chase it away. But if you have a pet-dog, it is treated as a member of the family. Some pet owners even insure their dogs, give medical attention, feed them with expensive meals, allow them in their living rooms and even cars. They take time to train their dogs to give them character and attitude. Pet-dogs sleep in comfortable places. I heard of a man in Lagos some years back who gave a befitting burial to his dog. Who will do all these to a strayed dog? Sonship when we pray is much more important than pet and owner's relationship.

Let me shock you, do you know that a baby, no matter how dirty he or she might be, can jump on the father even when he wears the finest of cloth and does not expect a true father to turn him or her down? We enjoy the same privilege when we sin and turn to God our father in genuine repentance. He overlooks our confessed sin and accept us as His children. In 1 John 2:1 the Bible says,

> *"My little children, I am writing you these things so that you may not sin. But if anyone does sin, we have an advocate with the Father – Jesus Christ the Righteous One." - KJV.*

God sees a regenerated child as joint heir with Jesus Christ. If that is the case, it means we have unhindered access to God when we pray. But we need genuine repentance and confession to God. The Bible says God is faithful and just to forgive our sins and clean us from all unrighteousness (1 John 1:9). However, this is not a license to continue in deliberate sin. We cannot continue to dwell and revel in sin and think we are covered by God's grace (Romans 6:1).

I dwell so much on this chapter because it is foundational to praying effectively. You cannot pray rightly when you do not have the right relationship with God. If God is your father, it makes it easier when you pray to Him.

HALLOWED BE YOUR NAME

We will consider the word hallow in this context to mean, reverently honour as holy. Jesus' teaching about prayer in this context is about the position of honouring our holy God or reverence for God in holiness when we pray. The word reverence in *Hebrew* is used sometimes in English Bible, especially KJV, to mean fear. But the Hebrew word for reverence in the context of prayer is *morah* which is different from *phobeo* that means to be terrified or frightened. The Bible says in 1 John 4:18,

"There is no fear in love, but perfect love casts out fear. For fear has to do with punishment, and whoever fears has not been perfected in love" – (ESV).

Hallowed be your name in this framework is about elevating God, praising, appreciating and blessing His name, exalting Him before we begin to ask for anything.

We need to understand that to adore, worship and praise God when we pray are potent strategies than just asking God for what we need when we pray. One can see the importance of bonding when we pray, from the word hallow. Those who truly understand the secret of prayers know that quality worship and praise precipitate profound prayers, just as a responsible, appreciative and respectful child will not go to the father starting with a request without first acknowledging him.

God desires that we learn to be thankful and worship Him for what He has done, has not done and what He will do. In Luke 17:11-19, the Bible talks about the importance of giving God glory. Only one of the 10 lepers Jesus healed, went back to thank Him and that was the only one who had double portion of healing. He was made whole. Being made whole here is like not having the marks of leprosy. Others who did not revere God for their healings only had their healings, they were not made whole.

As God's children, whatever we ask for in prayers, we must be conscious of the fact that humility and reverence for God is important. We must humble ourselves when we pray. Sometimes we display arrogance when we pray. We need to be confident when we pray knowing that whatever we ask we will receive. Nevertheless, we must know and acknowledge that whatever we receive through prayer to God is just by His grace and not by our eloquence and power.

We ask for anything and receive from God in the name of Jesus Christ, not because of our proficiency in prayer mannerism. The Bible says,

> *"Likewise, the Spirit also helpeth our infirmities: for we know not what we should pray for as we ought: but the Spirit 'himself' maketh intercession for us with groanings which cannot be uttered." –Romans 8:26 (KJV).*

This is a clear demonstration of the fact that it is not that we know how to pray but that we have an advocate in the person of Jesus Christ.

Most often we are too much in a haste to enjoy God's benevolence by rushing into asking and asking without spiritual worship and reverence for God. Worship is an essential part of our fellowship with God in prayers. You do not go to a court to talk to the judge anyhow. Lawyers address judges as lord. Even within the court premises, there is a limit to how loud you can talk, not to talk of the court room. When you address a judge, you do so with reverence. Even the lawyers, after referring to the judge as their lord, argue their cases with reverence. If your phone rings in the court room, you could be liable for an offense and charged with disrespecting the court and may be fined or even jailed.

Some Christians are used by God to perform miracles and they suddenly become proud as if they are the one performing the miracles which God has done in response to their prayers. When we pray, we must be conscious of the fact that the glory of answered prayers go back to God. We cannot afford to share in His glory when we have breakthrough in prayers.

If we truly reverence God, we will not allow distractions when we pray. Your phone or family should not come between you and God, your thoughts should not wander to mundane things. Remember, God sees your heart and seeks your total being and attention when you pray to him. Doubting God when we pray is tantamount to dishonouring him, belittling His ultimate power to do whatever pleases Him, including answering our prayers.

People sometimes behave in a way that makes it look like we respect man, our spouses, work, phone, etc. than God. We must make clear the supremacy of God to everyone in everything we do, including when we pray. Our family members must know that nothing can come between us and God when we pray. If we are in a meeting with important personalities, we cannot attend to phone calls. When we have an appointment with high dignitaries or people at that, we honour them by keeping to time. When you have fixed a time to pray to God, you need to keep to it. It is not what we wave with the back of our hands and conclude that God will understand when we go late to His. If He will understand anything, it should be that we honour our time and appointment with Him reverently.

YOUR KINGDOM COME

There are so many things the teaching of Jesus on this topic teaches. When we pray, if we know that God is sovereign and oversees everything as King, it gives us confidence and assurance that we are praying to the King who has a domain that has solutions to all we may have as challenges. God's domain is unlimited and has no boundary. This topic is assuring us that when we pray to God who has everything we may need, we need not worry about how the solution will come. No wonder, the Bible says,

> *"Now to Him who is able to do far more abundantly than all that we ask or think" Ephesians 3:20A (ESV).*

God has everything we need. All we need to do is to turn to Him in prayer. We do not need to seek for help from any other source and kingdom-less *kings*. Being connected to the Kingdom of God and benefitting from it require that we are first and foremost a citizen of the kingdom. He can make everything work if we belong to His kingdom, because He rules in the affairs of men. Your health condition, career, marriage, business, among others can be fixed by God who owns the heavenly and earthly kingdom. All you need is to discuss your case with Him when issues arise.

Our prayers must be tested with how the kingdom of God will feel about what we are asking for. We must measure whether the Kingdom of God will be happy answering our prayer or not. If God will respond to all our prayer requests, only few people will be left on earth by now, especially when we pray against our enemies. Heaven does not want the death of a sinner but that he or she should come to repentance. When we pray for the death of our enemies, God is looking at how to save the souls of such enemies. So, the Kingdom's view about our prayers is very important.

There are things we ask for in prayers, but God knows that if we have them, we may not be able to make it to His kingdom. So, He weighs our requests vis-à-vis what His kingdom holds for us. If our prayers must be answered, the content must be in line with what God's kingdom will approve of. I wonder if God will allow some of our prayer requests to get near His throne, especially weighing our motives for asking. There are selfish prayers we pray so fervently that can make God wonder if we know who He is and what he wants for us. One of God's kingdom test is love. Looking at some prayers we pray, can we really say they are borne out of love for God and others?

When we pray to God whose kingdom is saturated and enveloped with holiness, we need to have a heavenly ambience of holiness. The environment in which we pray, especially our heart must be holy. God's kingdom is holy, and our hearts, hands and lives must be that of holiness. In Psalm 24:3-4 the Bible says,

> *"Who shall ascend the hill of the LORD? And who shall stand in His holy place? He who has clean hands and a pure heart, who does not lift up his soul to what is false and does not swear deceitfully" –(ESV).*

No wonder, David asked God to create in him a clean heart – Psalm 51:10. Fellowship with God cannot be in an unholy atmosphere. Our fellowship with God should not be defined by time, just as it should not be limited to locations, His kingdom has no boundary. Therefore, we must be holy all the time in readiness to walk and talk with Him in prayers anywhere we find ourselves. Our hearts must be the residence of God. That is why the Bible says in 1 Corinthians 3:16,

"Do you not know that you are God's temple and that God's Spirit dwells in you? – ESV.

If we are the temple of God and the Holy Spirit dwells in us, we cannot accommodate impurity in any way. Therefore, by implication, we are ambassadors of God's kingdom here on earth if He dwells in us, and we carry His image with us anywhere we go. If He dwells in us, our prayer lives will make a lot of differences. It means we are constantly in tune with heaven in all we do. It is impossible to go wrong, with God in us. The Bible says Christ in you the hope of glory (Colossians 1:27B). In the Epistle of Paul to the Colossians, one of the key emphasis is for Christians to live in the world with heavenly focus and consciousness rather than being terrestrially fixated. It means whatever the outcome of our prayers may be, as far as God is glorified, we worry less.

When we pray in line with God's kingdom principles, the testimonies will be glorious. It means whatever answer we get when we pray, we are conscious of the truth that God will be glorified. Whether God says yes, wait or no to our prayers, a kingdom-minded person knows that God will be glorified at the end of it all. Such people are not perturbed when it seems the positive response to their prayers are seemingly delayed.

A taste of heaven or God's kingdom when we pray is in true worship. The Angels in heaven have the duty to worship and adore God always. One of the lessons we should learn from this teaching of Jesus is to be full of praises just like the Angels do in heaven. A life of praise in prayer is a life of victory and testimonies. God's kingdom-minded Christians praise God even when answers to their prayers are wait or no. They do not impose their wishes and will on God's will. They respect the will of God in everything they do.

YOUR WILL BE DONE ON EARTH AS IT IS IN HEAVEN

Obviously, doing God's will is not just an earthly requirement. The topic of this chapter as taught by Jesus shows that the will of God should be endemic and required both in heaven and on earth. There is an encouraging word in 1 John 5:14,

"And this is the confidence that we have in him, that, if we ask any thing according to his will, he heareth us" - (KJV).

Jesus talked agonisingly when He was faced with death. Seeing what was ahead of him – the scourge; the crown of thorn; being subjected to open shame; carrying the heavy cross; being spat on and mocked; crucifixion; being held by the cold hands of death; having to bear the past, present and future sin of mankind and being punished for it; and ultimately, being forsaken by His Father, an experience he had never had – his soul became "exceeding sorrowful" (Matt. 26:38, KJV). All these things and more, that we probably may not understand, except they are revealed to us by God, are put in a cup he would drink, i.e., he was to go through all these! He became so sad.

In that state of overwhelming sorrow, He prayed, "My Father, if it is possible, don't make me suffer by making me drink from this cup." (Matt. 26:39, CEV). Jesus prayed a prayer that God would not answer. Being the second person in the Godhead, Jesus was privy to the plan of redemption designed by God before the foundation of the earth for the redemption of mankind. This plan was not known to anyone else, not even the devil may know this, because if the devil had known, he would have done everything to stop Jesus from going to the cross (1 Cor. 2:8). What was about to happen was the most important event in the programme of heaven for mankind, the best of God's creation, centre of His love and pivot around which the entire creation revolves.

It was important and inevitable, but it involved Jesus being sacrificed as offering for the sin he did not commit. Jesus prayed. Have you ever wondered the implication of having that prayer answered? It means God's eternal plan would have been defeated. It means Jesus would have lived an unfulfilled life; he would have missed his destiny. It means he would not have gone to the grave. It means death, the grave and hell would have retained their powers. It means the devil would continually hold sway over human beings. It means there would be no name above every other name. It means there would be no provision for healing. It means there would be no salvation and we would have been eternally doomed. The implication is greater than what any of us could imagine.

Jesus probably remembered the implication of his request to let the cup pass over him, hence under the same breath, he added, "... nevertheless not as I will, but as thou wilt." (Matt. 26:39, KJV). He acknowledged God in that prayer as the omniscient, the all-knowing who knows the end from the beginning. He revealed God as one who has the best plan for his creature. Though we do not understand what He is doing, following Him, notwithstanding, is the best decision. It may not make sense in the immediate, it will eventually be the most sensible thing to do. Jesus submitted his desire to the will of the Father.

Dear reader, mankind has yet to recover from that singular decision – Jesus' decision to submit to the will of God, despite how

He felt. Jesus is not the only beneficiary of the tough choice He made. He went through it all and went to the grave to take the power of death and hell (Eph. 4:9; Rev. 1:18). All things became subject to Him and He was given a name that is above every other name (Eph. 1:19-22; Philippians 2:9-11). He rewrote history and the calendar being used today started counting from the sacrifice He offered. Even the countries that have different calendars only have them within their borders. Those calendars become secondary the moment they have cause to relate globally.

You are also a beneficiary of Jesus' submission. Whatever keeps you down is what you have allowed. Jesus has conquered EVERY-THING (note the emphasis). Everything means all inclusive, nothing excluded. The victory He got has been made available to you (1 Cor. 15:58). No work or power of the enemy or the devil can overcome you, except you allow it. We got all these just because Jesus said, thy will be done (Matt. 26:42). Can you just imagine how much you have been losing or you stand to lose by insisting before God that your own will must prevail?

There are other Bible characters who got the best because they settled for God's will and not theirs. But I have chosen to show you the biggest example, Jesus himself. He asked the father to let the cup of death pass over Him. But immediately, He said, but not my will but your (God's) will. Praying according to our needs most times may bring us against God's purpose and will for our lives. Jesus having taught his disciples the need for a relationship with God as a requirement to pray unto Him, the importance of reverencing Him (with our talent, time, treasure, knowing they are all from God). One may also interpret the key words in the topic of this chapter to also mean that when we pray, we need to be heavenly conscious in our communication with God, as we have seen in chapter five, knowing that some terrestrial benefits we receive from our father when we pray to Him, are not everlasting. Our requests in prayers must be tied to God's will and heavens prescriptions.

An effective prayer requires that our request is centred on God's will. Most of our prayers are unanswered just because we ask wrongly. Before we continue, let us ask what the prime will of God is. God has not hidden his will from us. He has given us precious promises in His word, showing us what He has prepared for us and what He expects our lives to look like. Praying based on any of His promises is praying according to His will. There are, however, other areas of lives where we must make specific decisions. We may have some things which are appealing to us but leaving such for what He will have us get means taking up His will. A doctor who has his own hospital may, for instance, want his son to be a doctor to inherit the hospital. He would be going against the will of God, if God has created the boy to be an athlete. The father needs to pray the prayer of Jesus – not as I will, but as you will.

Though the first man and woman lost eternity through disobedience to the commandment of God by the deception of Satan, God's love to mankind never ceases. One of His wills and the ultimate will is that no man is lost to the devil eternally. For effective prayer to be offered therefore, God desires that we are saved as earlier discussed in chapter three. Besides that, God has definite purpose and will for every man and woman which we must identify and stick to.

God's will must be identified when we pray before we go into any relationship, marriage or whatever; choose a career; accept an offer of appointment; rent an apartment; buy any property; or make any other quality life decision. Getting things right at the very beginning is foundational to subsequent prayer relationship we may want to have with God. If you ignore God from the beginning of any issue, bringing him in to rubber stamp it will be difficult to achieve.

We probably get entangled with some difficulties by not understanding what God's will is from inception when we have a decision to make. You may have erred foundationally and may be going through the punishment of not carrying God along. God is merciful, but you may have to live with some of the decisions taken outside the will of God. If you are married to someone without seeking to know God's will before starting off your courtship, God can only grant you the grace to cope with some experiences until He gives you solution. He will not ask you to divorce your spouse.

If our prayers must be effective, we must be prepared to ask for what the will of God is at every point of our decisions, be it spiritual or physical. The will of God requires holistic understanding. It may include:

Time

Jesus was taken to Egypt for fulfilment of time. God has specific time for everything He does and for things He would do for all His children. As humans, we may always be tempted to have things our own way, including time to do things. We want results now and now. But God, our father does not respond to all our requests with such instantaneity all the time. We may be in a certain situation when He promptly intervenes when we call on Him, but not all the time.

One of God's will for us is that we have things at the right time. In Ecclesiastes 3:17B the Bible says,

> *"... for there is a time for every matter and for every work" (ESV).*

For every prayer we offer to God, He has appropriate time in His schedule to answer them. We cannot cajole God to do what He knows will hurt us as His children; if He knows the timing is wrong, He will not do it. The will of God is that we have answers to our prayers.

So, when you pray, and it seems the result is not forthcoming, do not be discouraged, it may just mean that your Father's timing is different from yours. No good father will want to hurt His child just to please him or her with whatever he or she asks for without minding if such a child is ripe to have it or not. Even when God gave a vision to His Prophet Habakkuk, Habakkuk 2:3 says,

> *"For the vision is meant for its appointed time; it speaks of the end, and it does not lie; it may take a while, but wait for it; it will surely come, it will not delay" (Complete Jewish Bible – CJB).*

God has defined time for everything. To understand the will of God for timing when we pray, Ecclesiastes 3:1 to 8 lay emphasis on the importance of timing. God puts time to every of His purpose for us as His children and we need to understand this when we pray. Do not get into depression thinking God does not want to answer your prayers even when you have fasted and prayed like Daniel did for 21 days. God's time for your request is the best time for you to have His blessings without sorrow.

Purpose

Our creation and existence is for one purpose or another. The Bible says,

> *"I will not die, but I will live and proclaim what the LORD has done" (HCSB).*

When we pray for long life or anything, we need to understand that the will of God is that we use our lives and resources for His glory. Whatever a child of God is praying for, having it must be to help advance the cause of God's kingdom here on earth. Even our lives, fulfilling our days before we die, is to declare the works of

God.

So, when we pray for long life or anything at that, we must understand that God's answer has purpose attached to it. This is one of the reasons God does not answer some prayers. As Omniscient, He knows before we ask for anything if our intention or purpose for asking is carnal or if giving us what we ask for will be injurious to us, as such He may not grant our requests. So, when we want to pray effectively, we must align our purpose with that of God or His will for us.

Sometimes, we do ask in prayer for certain things, but they are at variance with what the purpose of God is for our lives. Even in ministry, as spiritual as issues might look, God has divine purpose for everyone He has called to ministry. Pursuing another person's calling will not bring fulfilment. Even in secular businesses, everyone has specific purpose for which he or she can add value to an organisation. God may not grant our request in prayer if we pray to fulfil another person's purpose. God's will for you has purpose embedded in it. When your prayer negates His will and purpose for you, God will not grant your prayer.

Place

Even though, God has all it took to protect Moses in the land of Egypt after his brethren accused him of killing an Egyptian, he fled from Egypt to a place of learning for another 40 years, leading animals. It was a period to learn patience. Sometimes, we leave God's location to our place of comfort where God's allocation may not be delivered to us. When you are where God does not want for you, your promotion and success may be delayed. God has assigned locations to excel to everyone, leaving such locations and praying to God for breakthrough may a be mere waste of time and energy.

Despite the famine in the land of the Philistines the Lord appeared to Isaac and told him not to go down to Egypt but to dwell in the land He would tell him. God instructed him to sojourn in Gerar, where he was, and that He would bless him (Genesis 26:1-6). Common sense will tell anyone to relocate from an economically recessed country to a booming and promising economy. But God told Isaac to remain in an economy that was gloomy. In verses 12 and 13 of Genesis 26, the Bible says,

> *"And Isaac sowed in that land and reaped in the same year a hundredfold. The LORD blessed him, and the man became rich, and gained more and more until he became very wealthy" – ESV.*

Mark it, the Bible did not say he became rich only, but that he became wealthy. To be rich is the elementary stage of blessing; to have financial freedom, the aspiration of everyone should be wealth and not just riches. Isaac had the mind of going down to Egypt, but he was divinely guided to remain where he was. Isaac never had such a bountiful harvest as he had that year – in a year and a land of famine. If he had left to where he thought there would be increase, God would have left him to work hard in his chosen location without anything to show for it.

My spiritual father, Bishop Francis Wale Oke told me on January 3rd, 2018, when he came to start off the year with us with sessions of prayers during our first working day in the office, that **when man works, man works, but when a man prays, God works**. Do not term this to mean having to stay idle and ask God to bless you. It will not work. Success and failure are worked for. However, success requires hard work, while failure requires indolence. God blesses what we invest our efforts to do. God's blessings multiplied by 0 due to laziness equals 0. You put in no efforts, God blesses nothing! Smartness, or whatever it is called, is no substitute for hard work. Enduring success is a product of hard work, God's wisdom and His multiple blessings.

When I listen to some supposed prophetic declarations on the television by Pastors, I wonder where the will of God is as they sanction the unguided and unguarded desire of some people to travel to other developed countries. It appears to me they are promoting a theology that is centred on human desire alone. They make it look as if people can only make it in life by travelling out of a non-functional country. Friends, I am not against relocating to another country, especially if things are not working in your country. But relocating to any place is a destiny issue, a decision that should not be taken outside God's will and guidance. Jesus' teaching on this topic is that our will, when we pray, should align with God's will for us.

Do not be cajoled into thinking that money is picked on the streets of London and New York. People work to make money in these countries. I must say that if some people can put in half of the energy and time they put into making a living out there in Europe and United States of America, they may be better off staying back in their countries. I pray that our leaders in the developing countries will one day make things work so that some who have left the shores of Africa will return home. The difference between the developed countries people run to and the underdeveloped or developing countries is that they have leaders, structures, systems and infrastructures that run according to biblical principles to make things easy for their citizens, even when some of them do not believe in or know God. Nevertheless, before you make the move to relocate within or outside your country, let God guide you with His will for your life. Do not pray to have anything or do anything outside of the will of God.

GIVE US THIS DAY OUR DAILY BREAD

This is one of the passages being misinterpreted by unbelievers. It may look awkward for someone who is seemingly financially buoyant to still pray for daily bread when he or she already has more than enough to eat. But Psalm 23 gives a clear clue to this issue of give us our daily bread. A shepherd daily takes out his flock seeking greener pasture for them. A shepherd is always seeking for the best for his flock. As a child of God, He seeks better deals for you day by day. Even if you have good food and good job, God, your Shepherd is thinking you need something better than the previous day every day of your life. When you can have something better than you had yesterday, why will you settle for something good?

It is a surface knowledge of this statement that will make people think one does not need God for his or her daily bread. God knows what is best for you and will want to daily lead you to the source of better things, if only you can rely on Him. When you are too wise and think because you have all you need now, you do not need God for your daily bread, it makes you settle for less than God's best for your life. I am sure you will want to settle for the best and not the good.

Interpreting daily bread to mean only physical food robs one of the deep knowledge and experience of what bread is. The Bible says,

"Man shall not live by bread (physical food) alone, but by every word (spiritual food) that comes from the mouth of God" – Matthew 4:4 (ESV).

Bread for our context will be viewed from both physical and spiritual dimension. Relying on spiritual nourishment of yesterday, makes one a malnourished Christian. As children of God, we need daily bread from God to be refreshed. To grow as children of God, we need to depend on God for daily portion of the bread from above.

A divinely inspired prayer requires that we continuously depend on the Holy Spirit to feed us with the needed spiritual nourishment that gives us spiritual alertness to pray rightly. David understood the importance of absolute reliance on God for daily bread. He defined the pasture that the figurative Shepherd (God) leads him to in Psalm 23. There are pastures and there are pastures. The Shepherd did not only lead David to a greener pasture but also to where there were still waters. Imagine eating balanced diet and refreshing yourself with water. The word pasture and water can stand alone without the premodifiers green and still. The emphasis here is that when we depend on God in our prayers and are led by the Holy Spirit, we do not get the ordinary things, we get the best.

The difference between the bread you have and the one you get when you depend on God's daily provision is that you eat the latter in the presence of your enemies without them being able to harm you. David says, in Psalm 23:5,

"You prepare a table before me in the presence of my enemies; you anoint my head with oil; my cup overflows – (ESV).

No wonder the Bible says,

> *"The blessing of the LORD makes rich, and he adds no sorrow with it" – Proverbs 10:22 (ESV).*

There is nothing your enemies can do when you get the blessings that come from God. When your daily portion of bread comes from God, you are refreshed more than when you are fed with bread of sorrow from man. Can you see why through prayer, you need to rely on God for your daily provision?

Give us our daily bread as used in this passage teaches absolute dependence on God for our daily supply beyond food. Ignorantly, a rich man once mocked Christians who pray for God's daily supply. He argued that he had more than enough food in his store that could last him for months and as such does not see the need to ask God for daily supply. How I wish someone could inform him that the health with which he pursues wealth daily, which has enabled him to have abundance of food in his home, was given by God. I believe God must have a reason for not proving Himself to the ignorant man as he did with the man in the Bible who depended on his affluence and boasted to pull down his ban and rebuild it to enable his soul to dine and wine. The Bible described him as a foolish man, as his soul was required of him that night.

Jesus taught His disciples just as He is teaching us today that praying to God is about identifying that we need Him for everything. This does not mean you lack physical supplies. You may have all you need but knowing that God is your only and ultimate source is very important. No one can have anything except it is given to him from above. This is where unbelievers get it wrong. They ascribe their possessions to their ability and efforts. Of course, everyone needs to work hard to make it in life, but without God's blessing, one's effort becomes meaningless.

Permit me to say that the understanding those who think they are sufficient and do not need to depend on God for their daily bread lack is that God has the power to make rich or make poor. The Bible says in 1 Samuel 2:7,

> *"The LORD makes poor and makes rich; He brings low and He exalts – (CEV).*

This verse I will interpret to mean that, whatever efforts we make to be rich, only God can make it work. If He does not bless our efforts, there is nothing anyone can do to be rich. That we have food to eat, therefore, is simply by God's grace and blessing. The blessing may be out of God's general or specific benevolence.

FORGIVE US OUR DEBTS AS WE FORGIVE OUR DEBTORS

The parable of the unforgiving servant as recorded in the Gospel of Matthew 18:21-35 describes aptly the importance of forgiveness in prayer. Jesus started the passage in answer to Peter's question on how often he (Peter) would forgive his brother. Jesus told Peter that he should forgive his brother, seventy-seven times. It sounds incredible for anyone to give himself to being offended that number of times and even counting, anyway. Jesus concluded the parable by telling Peter that God will treat anyone who fails to forgive wholeheartedly like the unforgiving servant who was jailed for not forgiving his debtor after his own debt was forgiven. If such a punishment could be meted out by God for unforgiveness, how then will an unforgiving person pray to God and expect positive answer from Him?

According to *greekwordstudies.blogspot.com*, one of the translations or meaning of the word "forgive" in Greek is *charizomai* from the root word *charis* which means grace. The word used in this form appeared many times in the New Testament. This is about unmerited and unrestricted forgiveness. God requires that we forgive those who sin against us unconditionally even when they do not deserve it, just as God demonstrated towards us, that even when we were yet sinners, Christ died for us - Ephesians 4:32; Colossians 2:13 and 3:13. Forgiveness is not an easy thing to do. No wonder it is said that to revenge is natural, but to forgive is divine. Christ taught His disciples that one of the requirements to pray and by extension to pray effectively is to learn and choose the path of forgiveness.

Looking at the seminar of Jesus on prayers, having finalised His teachings, one thing He emphasized was forgiveness. In Matthew 6:14-15 He makes it clear that when we do not forgive others, God will not forgive us. How then can we pray to God and expect Him to answer our prayers when we habour unforgiveness? It means we are disconnected from the throne of grace when we are unable to forgive anyone that offends us. To obtain forgiveness even from God, Jesus said in Mark 11:25,

"And when you stand praying, forgive, if you have anything against anyone, so that your Father also who is in heaven may forgive your trespasses – ESV.

I am not sure if you can see what I am seeing here. This verse exposes with certainty that the sin of unforgiveness could be committed by even careless Christians. Jesus refers to children of God in this passage when He said, *so that your Father...* God cannot be called your Father if you are yet to be born again. No wonder, so many prayers of Christians are not effective because they harbour unforgiveness. The sin of unforgiveness is not different from the sin of witchcraft. The gravity of this verse is that, when you fail to forgive, your role in the church and title notwithstanding, God will not forgive your sins also.

Many tongue blasting and prayerful Christians may need to pay serious attention to this aspect of Christ's teaching. Forgiveness is important and central to answered prayers. We cannot keep grudge or harbour unforgiveness and expect God to listen to our prayers, let alone answer them positively. The prayer of an unforgiving man is irritant to God. Can you just pause and think about those you may be holding grudges against and take steps to reconcile with them before continuing with the reading of this book?

Unforgiveness goes beyond hindering your prayers, it could be a reason for not making heaven. Remember this, you suffer both physically and spiritually for not forgiving those who have sinned against you. You may have health complications and you are also disconnected from God. Meanwhile, the person you are holding grudge against may not even remember he or she has offended you.

Many Christians including church leaders are struggling with unforgiveness. We may have genuine reasons for harbouring unforgiveness, but they are not enough reasons for God not to reject our prayers. For example, it is not an easy thing for a Pastor to have laboured for years to gather members only for a young dynamic and charismatic Pastor to cause a break-away by scattering such a congregation, taking some away through malicious lies. Yet, not forgiving even under such circumstance constitutes serious barrier to effective prayers.

How about when a faithful wife discovers that the husband has been unfaithful, having a child out of wedlock or the husband discovers that the paternity of one of his children is not his? How do you forgive under such circumstance? But holding to grudges for any reason at that, constitutes serious strain to relating with God in prayers. We just must learn forgiveness to pray effectively. The devil understands how potent this sin is and uses it consistently to hold down many professing Christians.

DO NOT LEAD US TO TEMPTATION

Temptation is an invitation to commit sin. It is not a sin to be tempted but yielding to temptation is sin. But even when one has overcome a temptation, the devil will always come back with another. He tempted Jesus even at a time when one would have expected him not to go near Jesus. Jesus just concluded a forty-day and night fast. Ordinarily, that could mean a ferocious time to cross Jesus' path as one would assume He would be tough for the devil to handle. The devil came to Him in three ways that are still potent areas of temptation for Christians today.

Satan used and is still using the lust of the flesh (food), the lust of the eyes (beautiful things) and pride of life (power) as in 1 John 2:16 to tempt. He tempted Jesus with food, knowing he was hungry, after 40 days and night of dry fast (Matthew 4:2). He tempted him with beautiful things of the world and thirdly with power. Do not trust a man to be humble until you give him power and it is not misused. Jesus passed the three temptations, but the devil left Him only for a while.

As a Christian, are you aware that the devil is always out to tempt you as a strategic weapon to keep you busy with sin and separate you from God in the place of prayer? He knows God hates sin and His eyes are too holy to behold iniquities and will ever keep trying to seduce one to sin. The devil knows that when he succeeds in making you yield to temptation, he will succeed to separate you from the place of prayer and before God, even if it is for a short time or permanently.

Therefore, Satan will never give up trying until he achieves his purpose of luring one to sin. I pray Satan will never overcome us in the place of prayer through yielding to his antics to sin in Jesus' name. When we fast and pray and yet discover that it is usually then we are tempted with sin of all sort, it is not a new strategy, the devil will come to tempt us with the intent to make us sin. We need to resist him through the power of the Holy Spirit.

The statement in the Lord's prayer, lead us not to temptation should not be termed that God will tempt His children with sin. The Bible says, God does not tempt anyone as we are tempted out of the multitude of the desires in our heart (James 1:12-15; Romans 7:5). God does not tempt anyone with sin. This topic is a call to children of God to know that temptation is a steady strategy of Satan to make one to sin. No wonder Jesus made it an area of attention if we would be able to pray effectively. When you are kept away from sin, you can be sure your relationship with God will be smooth.

A Christian's life is supposed to be consistently devoid of sin that could result from temptation. Prayer is a process of communication by which we relate with God. Jesus teaching us to pray that we are not led into temptation is a warning that we should consciously abstain from things, places, people, etc. that could make us susceptible to sin. Children of God should live a life of prayer and not only pray for a number of times in a day. Of course, we must have dedicated time for fellowship with God in prayers, but praying is a lifestyle that helps us throughout the day, communicating with our Father. This is where Christians should be different by not doing mechanistic praying.

Naturally, a child of God should wake up praying; go to office/ school/market/ praying; about to drive off from one point to another, you are praying; you get to the office or your destination, you are praying; you are offered food, you pray; you close from work, you pray; you are driving home, you are praying; you get home, you are praying; a question is posed to you by someone and you find yourself praying before giving a response; you want to go to bed, you are praying. It is difficult for a child of God to count the number of times he or she prays in a day. Therefore, yielding to temptation will break our relationship and communication with God which could be dangerous. The devil looks for such opportunity to hit Christians.

Jesus is teaching us here to abstain from whatever could lead us to temptation and invariably yielding to temptation. Yielding to temptation will hinder our spiritual flow with our Father when we communicate with Him. In Genesis 3:8 the Bible says,

> *"And they heard the sound of the LORD God walking in the garden in the cool of the day, and the man and his wife hid themselves from the presence of the LORD God among the trees of the garden" (ESV).*

Adam and Eve were having sweet fellowship with God and communicating with Him freely until they disobeyed God by yielding to the temptation of the devil. They hid themselves from God. Covering up when we sin has been humans' strategy. Hiding behind one finger, how thoughtless could sin make man look? Had Adam and Eve forgotten that God sees everything around the world? How will they ever think they could hide from God. But that is what Satan does. He makes us look for cover up instead of confessing our sins. Some even go to the extent of telling lies to cover up or giving excuses for sinning. Adam played the blame game, he blamed God for giving him a helper. The wife Adam once cherished and called bone of his bone and flesh of his flesh suddenly became the woman God gave to be with him, no longer wife.

Jesus in His teachings on temptation opened our minds to the truth that we should not go near whatever could make us to be tempted to sin, as it cuts us from God our Father. Watch the environment you stay, where you go alone and what time you go to sin-prone areas. You will not be tempted with things you cannot feel, see, think or hear about. Going to spiritually contaminated places or moving with people who will make you susceptible to temptation should be avoided as a child of God.

DELIVER US FROM THE EVIL ONE

In John 10:10a, the Bible says, the thief comes only to steal, kill and destroy. He has agents in different forms and always does everything to steal the fervency of prayers. He uses diverse strategic approaches to kill the potency of prayers. This is one of the reasons we must not only be prayerful but watchful. No wonder, Jesus warned the three disciples He took with Him to the Garden of Gethsemane that they should watch and pray so as not to fall into temptation (Matthew 26:41).

The syntax and synchronization in the statement by Jesus to His disciples to watch and pray and not to pray and watch have instructive significance. The devil is conscious of the fact that prayers offered by the children of God is fervent and potent. One major weapon of Satan to dissuade effective praying is by making a child of God to commit sin and fail to repent of it. Or make a Christian to be weak in prayer or not pray at all. By that, Satan achieves his purpose.

Jesus having realised the antics of Satan, in His teaching on how to pray, instructed his disciples to pray for deliverance from the evil one. The most potent strategy of the devil is not to kill a person, but that he does everything possible to separate Christians from relating with their Father (God) in prayers. The watchfulness Jesus talks about above in the Gospel of Matthew is about staying awake, agile, active, not dosing off spiritually. If you are going to win the devil in the place of prayer, you must be sensitive to every of his strategy and distraction. There is a saying in the western part of Nigeria that for one not to see evil, alertness – physical, mental and spiritual – is the solution. To be delivered from the tricks of Satan, we need to be conscious of everything he may device to overcome us in the place of prayer.

A strong weapon of the devil we need to be delivered from if we must pray effectively is arrogance. When the devil cannot arrest you with common sins, he stirs up the giant of pride in you. Satan knows that God hates arrogance. It was one of the reasons God drove Satan from heaven as written in Isaiah 14:12-19. The devil allows you to start small and devote good time to building a strong relationship with God. But when you become too strong for him, he makes you think you are an achiever and deceives you to disregard God's enablement. No wonder, we hear great ministers of the gospel claiming to be able to heal and deliver. They have taken the position and glory of God in their ministries. God does not share His glory with anyone. Therefore, as you grow strong and want to keep getting stronger in your relationship with God, please always ask God to deliver you from the evil one. Pray never to be arrogant when your spiritual life blossoms.

Before I became the Chief Executive Officer of the last organisation I have worked with for 18 years in 2013, I was praying and got an inspiration not to see myself as the one who would make things happen in the organisation. I was inspired and instructed that God is the leader who only requires my partnership and the moment I see myself as the one doing the stuff, I would start to fail. In less than three years of my appointment, God achieved through our team unprecedented successes in the history of the organisation.

In the centre of the euphoria of what God has achieved through us there was a serious economic recession that had not been witnessed for decades before 2016. The recession tore apart great companies, even some States of the federation could not pay salaries for months. We could not get forex to bring Bibles into Nigeria. We were humanly and literally helpless. My leadership ability could not help me out, I kept praying to God to see the organisation through the hard time and help us not to lay off any staff member. He answered the prayers.

Why the story, if the devil uses gentle approaches to dissuade you from effectively praying, he could go violent to make you lose your cool and probably start looking for help where there is no help. However, if you have built a relationship with God, tough times will come which may require you praying like never. Amid this, it may seem as if God is far from you but note that this is the antics of the devil to distract you from effective praying. Keep at praying, relate well with God and He will deliver you from the evil one.

Effective prayer life requires constant understanding of the devil's strategies to distract from effective praying. This explains why Jesus taught His disciples to pray for God to deliver them from the evil one. Never underrate the extent the devil can go with you to discourage your sweet relationship with God but remember God has not given him the power to overcome you. Remember that every ploy of the devil is an attempt to strain your relationship with God, thus rendering praying ineffective.

YOURS IS THE KINGDOM AND THE POWER AND THE GLORY

The teaching of Jesus on this topic is directly or indirectly guiding us to have faith and trust in God when we pray because of His omnipotence. As a King, He has the kingdom. He has ultimate power and glory belongs to Him when He answers our prayers. To pray effectively, an effective prayer warrior or intercessor must understand the three key concepts in this topic – kingdom, power and glory. Jesus' teaching here shows that there are kingdoms that want to interfere in the prayer domain, but the Kingdom is of God. The interference of other kingdoms in the place of prayer is a dissuading strategy, but they can only overcome if one gives in to sin. The interference of the devil in Daniel's 3 weeks of communication with God is a good example of how kingdoms step in to create communication barrier when we pray.

As we discussed in Chapter 5, the kingdom of God has holiness as one of its principles and one needs to ask that God's kingdom would come. However, there is one vital implication in the words of Jesus here: For thine is *the* kingdom (Matt. 6:13, KJV). The article *the* used in that verse is instructive. A kingdom is the domain of a king. Everyone who has a domain, therefore, is a king in his own right and has a kingdom. That shows that there are many kingdoms. Within a kingdom, the king has the final say. God does not have a kingdom but THE kingdom, i.e. His is the only true kingdom. Other kingdoms are limited by one thing or the another – time, space, wealth, military might, geographical boundary and many more. The kingdom of God is not limited and cannot fall. It is eternally solid, stable and strong.

Talking about power as in the topic of this chapter depicts that there are powers but there is the ultimate Power, the power of God. Every other power is a counterfeit, nevertheless, Satan has the potential to derail prayers through sin. When Moses was sent to deliver the Israelites from the hand of Pharaoh and his kingdom, God used Moses to demonstrate His power to Moses in a bid to make him release His children, but Pharaoh's magicians counterfeited the original power.

When you are praying, the devil has a way of using his counterfeit power to appear real to make you believe God is not sufficient to be relied on as the only source of your power. When you bow to the devil's deception, he holds you captive. The Bible says in Romans 14:11A,

> *"As I live, says the Lord, every knee shall bow to me, and every tongue shall confess to God" – ESV.*

To effectively pray, we need the power of God. Prayer is not by human mechanistic power but by the power of God through His spirit. In this teaching of Jesus on prayer to His disciples, He said that the glory is God's. What does this teach us? When we pray and get results, the glory goes to God. Getting what we desire when we pray requires praying rightly and there is no doubt about that, but this does not come because of our eloquence. It is not by our righteousness even though righteousness is an essential ingredient when we pray. We must learn to give glory to God when He answers our prayers.

If God chooses not to answer prayers according to our requests there is nothing we can do than to align with His will. So, when we have miracles or breakthrough in prayers, God alone deserves the glory which we must never share with Him. We must remind ourselves that a breakthrough not well managed after answered prayers could be a hinderance to our future relationship with God. God will never share His glory with anyone.

CONCLUSION

We have made prayers look so complex that it is no longer a two-way communication that should exist between a father and a child. We believe that until certain categories of people pray for us, until we pray assuming certain postures or in some ways, or until we get to certain prayer locations, God will not answer our prayers. These are deceits of certain unbiblical theology. God will hear our prayers wherever we pray, whatever position we adopt. What is important is that we have a direct link with God in holiness and praying in line with His will. Do not misunderstand me. There is nothing wrong in joining our faith with those of our pastors and any child of God in prayer. The Bible says one will chase a thousand and two, ten thousand. So, there are battles we may need to fight in agreement with other children of God.

There are still true Pastors that we can relate with in our Christian journey. However, everything is wrong when we turn anyone to become a prayer contractor and deny ourselves direct access to God. Some cannot even do anything without consulting Pastors. This is prayer enslavement. When Jesus went to the cross, the veil of the temple was rent to give us direct access to God. The Bible calls us Royal Priesthood, while Jesus is our High Priest. The issue with some Christians is that they are too lazy, and they live below God's expectation. This laziness creates a sort of barrier between them and God when they pray.

Linking Phone Terminologies and Prayers

Let us use the phone terminologies to highlight some key issues in prayer as we conclude. This may look like an unconventional approach to conclude a spiritual text, but I believe using what we experience around us almost every day will help to drive home the point.

Dialling a Number. Every country on the globe has a dialling code. You cannot be in Nigeria and dial United States of America or any country at that without first using the right dialling code that connects you. Communicating with God requires a code. Holiness is the code. You can never have access to the number of God when you pray, unless you dial using the right code. When you try to make a call with the wrong code or number, you are not going to get through to your desired recipient.

The responses you are likely to get when the dialled number and code are wrong are; the number you are calling is incorrect, please check the number and dial again; or the number you are calling is not allocated. There are many reasons why a dialled number could be wrong when you pray. If you do not pray according to the will of God or have the right frame of mind, your call will get a wrong response. When you ask wrongly in prayer, you may be told you are dialling an unallocated number. So, when you pray, be sure you have the right code and number to get undeniable access to God.

Opening Salutation. In phone mannerism, you do not call a number and go into communication without a form of salutation. Praying to God requires starting with an expression of adoration to God. Those who understand the secret of prayers know that praise and worship is central to reaching the heart of God. Praise and worship prepare and usher us to the throne of grace. Our thanksgiving should be more than our requests when we pray. The challenge we have sometimes is that we are too much in a haste to ask God for what we need than to praise and adore Him. When you lack phone ethics of opening your discussion with politeness and greetings, you may not have good reception from your recipient. When you pray, start with quality praise and worship to unlock heaven.

Network Connection. Getting connected to any number is dependent on maybe you have a network provider or not. No matter the quality of your phone or the credit on it, you are never going to get through to your intended recipient without going through the right network provider. When Christ is not in your life, you will continuously experience failed calls to God when you pray because you are not going through the right network to heaven. Jesus is the network through which effective prayers can be offered. If you only use Jesus Christ's name when praying without Him in you, your call will always fail to connect because you are out of the network area.

Praying effectively requires that the Network Provider (Jesus) is within your radius of call, i.e., Christ is in you always. It is also possible because you are out of network coverage area, you may never have connection to get through to your intended recipient. As a Christian, there are businesses you cannot do, there are places you cannot go, there are people you cannot marry or keep company with, or else you will be out of network coverage area. When you pray in such businesses, locations, marriage or relationship, you are not going to find it easy connecting with God as the Network Provider has no business being with you in such locations or situations. Every communication effort on a disconnected network is nothing but wasted effort, until you are rightly connected to the network. No matter the seriousness you put in when praying without being connected to the right Network, it is effort in futility.

Network failure happens for many reasons. It could be because of weather challenge, equipment breakdown, congestion due to high traffic at a point in time. Talking about prayer, sin is a network destroyer. It could be any kind of sin – unforgiveness, pride, fraudulent practice, fornication, etc. There is no small sin. When you pray, sin constitutes network congestion, thus delaying your prayer from getting through the Network (Jesus). What sin does to prayer is to cut the line of communication with God and kill the effectiveness of prayer. The Bible says in James 5:16,

"Therefore, confess your sins to one another and pray for one another, that you may be healed. The prayer of a righteous person has great power as it is working" (ESV). The KJV says, *"...The effectual fervent prayer of a righteous man availeth much."*

This passage is emphasising the power of sin to hinder an effective prayer and the need to rid oneself of sin before and after praying to God. Our Lord's prayer also teaches us the same thing, as we need to be sure sin is not hibernating in any corner of our lives when we pray. Sin collapses the effectiveness of the prayer apparatus. It starts by weakening prayer life and prayer itself, until it destroys it totally.

The Number You Are Calling Is Not Responding. From experience, when you make calls, the intended recipient maybe available or unavailable to receive your call. You might be able to get through, and yet receive a response that the intended recipient is not responding. When we pray, it is not every prayer that gets positive response instantly. This should teach us a lesson that God may choose not to give us what we asked for immediately, despite receiving our calls in prayers. He decides when to grant our requests. That someone has not responded to a call does not mean he or she may not respond. You just need patience. So, when you pray, know that God may have heard your prayer but He is only waiting to respond at the right time, a time which will not be injurious to you physically, spiritually and in every area of your life.

Patience is one of the virtues Christians must have as it gives us experience and character in our Christian journey – Romans 5:4-5. When you patiently wait for God's response, it builds your character which produces hope that does not bring shame to you as a Christian. Since patience builds one's character, it works out to make one a perfect Christian – James 1:4

Missed Call. I assume you know that when someone misses a call, it does not mean that the person was not available to answer the call. Sometimes, it may just be that the call is ignored. People may not answer calls for different reasons. But usually, people with intimate relationships will hardly ignore one another's call. If for any reason they are unable to respond to a call, they call back at the slightest opportunity.

When we pray without the right relationship with God or ask God for something for selfish use, He may ignore our calls. This is not to say that God is too busy to attend to the calls of everyone, but when the prayer is out of context or the one praying has no relationship with Him, He may not respond to the prayers. You can minimise your missed calls to heaven if you are always on the right Network and in right standing. There is a direct line to God, only the people with right standing in holiness have such number and code.

You Have Been Barred from Calling this Number. There are situations when one may bar a person from calling his or her number. Of course, abuse of relationship could be a reason to do such. Every relationship has its guiding principles. When we pray to God, there are principles we must adhere to. The most important is holiness check. When one's spiritual life has degenerated to unrepentant living, such a person's prayer call may be barred from getting access to the throne of God. King Saul in the Bible is an example of someone whose call was barred from God's presence. The Bible says,

"And when Saul, inquired of the LORD, the LORD did not answer him, either by dreams, or by Urim, or by prophets – 1 Samuel 28:6 (ESV).

Saul was confronted with a battle that required him to get direction from God, but He could not get God to communicate with him. That led Saul to multiply his sin before God. Saul went back to his vomit. He once got rid of witches from the land of Israel, but when he was denied access to God, he turned to the wrongs he once abhorred. No wonder, we have Pastors that heaven has rejected and barred from calling God, but to make up, they rely on other ungodly means to cover up, even though they still pray publicly in the name of Jesus. They perform fake miracles and people rush to them for prayers and divination.

Every child of God should be able to talk with God unhindered and without relying on Prophets who promise quick help but may not have access to heaven again. They resort to cloning the code of heaven by still calling on Jesus' name to deceive unsuspecting people. Resorting to self-help when unable to reach the throne of grace is compounding the whole issue. Seeking God in genuine repentance is the only option to have one's number removed from the barred list of numbers. God is merciful and gracious to forgive if we confess and forsake our sins.

Internet Enabled Phone. To get connected to an internet, one needs an internet enabled phone. No matter how high the level of internet connectivity in an environment is, if one's phone is not internet enabled, he cannot be connected. As a Christian, apart from having the right Network, our effectiveness in praying requires that we are wired to connect and that we are enabled. Prayer is not a mechanical process. We need the divine enablement through the Holy Spirit. The Bible says in Romans 8:26,

"Likewise the Spirit helps us in our weakness. For we do not know what to pray for as we ought, but the Spirit Himself intercedes for us with groanings too deep for words" (ESV).

Praying requires that one be guided by the Holy Spirit. Eloquence does not count in praying. The preciseness of prayer is guaranteed when inspired by the Holy Spirit. You can never go wrong with the Holy Spirit teaching you how to pray. Strength to pray and pray through in Jesus' name comes from the Holy Spirit.

Voice Mail. When someone does not want call access for any reason personal or official, they devise means that direct calls into voice mail. Voice mail does not mean your call will not be heard, it only means that your message cannot be responded to as at the time of making the call. Are you so eager about getting an answer from God about certain things? He may slow down responding to some of your requests in your own interest. God has the power to answer every prayer request immediately they are offered, but He may choose not to give immediate response for reasons best known to Him. Who knows, if God had answered that your pressing request, you might have died or quitted the faith.

Therefore, when it looks like your prayer has gone to the voice mail, it is not a denial, but a way God has chosen to answer your prayers in a way that glorifies Him and blesses you. Do not be too much in a hurry to get affirmative answers to your prayer all the time. When answers to some requests are delayed, wait and possibly ask God to reveal the reasons He chose not to respond immediately. This is why prayer should be a dialogue and not a monologue – a father and child communication.

Insufficient Credit or Data. Have you experienced insufficient fund to make calls, sometimes very important calls? You may even have started the conversation and reached a very important point and you are cut off. How painful could that be? In praying to God, one may run out of credit. One disgusting thing insufficient credit or data does is to deny you access to making calls or the internet. Secondly, it cuts you off during a serious discussion or usage. In any of these situations, you are ready to communicate, you have a strong network, your recipient is ready to speak with you, but you have insufficient credit or data on your phone.

Can we think about the Parable of the 10 virgins in the Bible as recorded in Matthew 25:1-13? Five were wise, but five were foolish. Praying requires wisdom that can only be given by the Holy Spirit. Everything may be set for effective prayer, but we are just limited by our knowledge of the Word of God, or absence of the Holy Spirit in us. The five unwise virgins planned and prepared like the others, but they lacked the wisdom to do just the extra thing, taking with them extra oil in case the groom tarries. Their oil burnt out, they missed it.

Can you remember how many times the devil tried Jesus after He had fasted and prayed for forty days and night? Imagine if Jesus had the right response for just the first or second temptation? You need enough Word of God in you to face every situation. You need to be able to tell the devil it is written for every situation that he brings your way when you pray. You cannot have enough credit or data if you do not invest money to get such. The same way, as a child of God if you do not invest enough time to reading, studying and meditating on the Word of God daily, you may run out of credit or data when praying.

When you face crushing situations in prayer, aside the grace of God, we need to develop ourselves and be deep in His Word. The Bible says in Colossians 3:16A,

"Let the Word of Christ dwell in you richly...." - (ESV).

God knows you need more of His Word in you as you grow in faith. How will you feel as a parent if your child does not grow to handle difficult situations that are commensurate with his or her age? Please wise up. Be filled with faith, the Holy Spirit and the Word of God. These are your credit and data in communicating with your Father.

When you are deficient in the essential ingredients of prayer, you may be cut off in the middle of serious communication with God in prayers. When you are supposed to be cracking bones, you cannot remain at the level of drinking milk and expect the devil to respect you. There are situations God expects you to handle by only giving thanks and commanding in the name of Jesus, not long prayers, to prove to Satan that you are a legitimate child of God. Of course, I must say that short prayers that produces public results, is a result of effective praying time in your closet.

I must say that going the whole haul with the devil and his agents requires that your credit and data have been recharged to premium level with the Network provider that could give you a roll-over credit which prevents you from running out of credit even when what you have paid for has been exhausted – that is grace. Jesus did not have to do intensive prayer before solving problems during His earthly ministry. When He was to raise Lazarus from the dead in John 11:41, He only said,

"Father, I thank you that you have heard me" – (ESV). Thereafter, He commanded Lazarus to come out of the grave. There was so-lution to the problem at hand just by Him giving thanks to His Father.

My friend, such praying strategy requires having sufficient credit with God, by the quality time you have spent in the closet during your private and quiet time with God, the depth of God's Word in you and your being filled with the Holy Spirit. One cannot be spending all his or her on things with less spiritual value and ex-pect God to work with him or her as He did with Jesus.

Can you remember what happened to the sons of Sceva in Acts 19:11-16? They had no credit to connect with God but wanted to cast out demon in the name of the God of Paul. That was a dangerous adventure. They were lucky to have gotten just the lit-tle beatings they got. Paul had credit with the Network provider and connection with heaven which empowered him to cast out demons, but that credit was not meant for the seven sons of Sceva the Jewish High Priest. In prayer, you cannot borrow credit from anyone, you need to have your own credit.

When people give testimonies about how they were faced with difficult situations and they used the name of the God of their Pastor to confront the situation, I wonder if they knew there is need for them to have their own credit to make call to God. Faith in man is not the same as faith in God. When will someone pray in the name of your own God? By implication, when you pray like that, you are only saying you do not have or that you have a limited relationship with the God of your Pastor. When will you be able to pray like your Pastor to unlock situations? Using another man's credit to make calls will rob you of ample time to talk. The same thing will happen if you depend on the connection of another believer to pray to God. You are limited in conversation when you borrow credit.

Thanks for taking out time to read this book on prayers. I pray that your prayer life will take a new turn for good in Jesus' name. Remember, it is essential that you are a child of God to have direct access to Him through Jesus Christ His son. Remain blessed.

ACKNOWLEDGEMENT

First and foremost, I appreciate God for His grace upon my life to write this book. I must say that writing this book took me such a long time than necessary due to exigencies of work, but God has made it possible for me to complete it.

I acknowledge the spiritual leaders whom God has used to nurture me since I gave my life to Christ 18th August, 1985. They have deposited in me nourishing spiritual food that has helped my growth in Christ.

I equally appreciate my family members, especially my wife and children who have been of tremendous support to me in every area of my life which has made it possible for me to achieve another feat of writing this book. My immense appreciation also goes to my colleagues at The Bible Society of Nigeria, Mr. Segun Obadare who proofread this book, Pastor Femi Akindele who designed the cover and Mrs. Grace Benjamin who typeset the initial draft of the book.

ABOUT THE AUTHOR

Richard Dare Ajiboye

Richard Dare Ajiboye, a holder of Doctor of Business Administration degree from Swiss Management Centre University, Switzerland, also holds an MA in Theology. He is a Certified Professional Coach and Licensed Human Resource and General Management Practitioner. Dare, a Fellow of the Chartered Institute of Administration; Nigerian Institute of Management and Nigerian Institute of Strategic Management, is also a Full Member of the Chartered Institute of Personnel Management, Nigeria. He is a Motivational and Public Speaker that has spoken in conferences and facilitated workshops in countries across Africa, Asia, Europe and Central America. So far, Ajiboye has authored 11 books and co-authored others.

BOOKS BY THIS AUTHOR

Lazarus Chose To Be Poor

This book is about our choices in life and building effective relationship. When opportunities are abused or not utilised, they become liabilities.

BOOKS BY THIS AUTHOR

Evergreen Words Of Wisdom

This book gives over 140 quotable quotes that touches virtually every aspects of human life.